inspirations

CROSS STITCH

Over 20 decorative projects for the home

inspirations

CROSS STITCH

Over 20 decorative projects for the home

LESLEY STANFIELD

PHOTOGRAPHY BY MICHELLE GARRETT

STEP-BY-STEP PHOTOGRAPHY BY MARK WOOD

LORENZ BOOKS

NEW YORK • LONDON • SYDNEY • BATH

This edition first published in 1997 by Lorenz Books
27 West 20th Street, New York, New York 10011

LORENZ BOOKS are available for bulk purchase for sales promotion and for premium use.
For details, write or call the manager of special sales:
Lorenz Books, 27 West 20th Street, New York, New York 10011; (800) 354–9657

© Anness Publishing Limited 1997

Lorenz Books is an imprint of
Anness Publishing Limited

ISBN 1 85967 534 4

Publisher: Joanna Lorenz
Senior Editor: Clare Nicholson
Designer: Bobbie Colgate-Stone
Photography: Michelle Garrett
Step-by-step photography: Mark Wood

Printed and bound in Hong Kong

1 3 5 7 9 10 8 6 4 2

CONTENTS

INTRODUCTION

CROSS STITCH was among the first embroidery stitches that I learnt at school, along with back stitch and blanket stitch. I attempted small designs in cross stitch to decorate egg cosies that we made, but that is as far as my embroidery skills advanced. I am very grateful that I was not brought up in the eighteenth and nineteenth centuries when producing a sampler to a standard beyond my wildest dreams was expected of a young girl.

To stitch cross stitch is simplicity itself; it is the design and the fineness of the thread used that adds the complexity. Of course I want to tackle projects such as decorating bedlinen, which would be a real labour of love, but I am not skilled enough to attempt such a large project straight away. For this reason, I will be starting with some of the smaller projects in this book. We have included projects that are small, simple and easy to achieve, working up to more complex designs. We show you how to work on canvas as well as how to work on fine materials. There is a full set of charts at the rear of the book as well as step-by-step instructions on how to make up your projects into items that range from a pincushion to decorating a simple curtain.

I hope that you catch the bug and stitch the sampler included in this book so that you will have a piece of embroidery that you are really proud of.

Deborah Barker

HOME SWEET HOME

This is a picture of a Victorian house and stands four-square, looking almost Shaker in its simplicity. Most styles of architecture would suit this treatment and you could produce a portrait of your own home by translating the essentials from a photograph onto graph paper to make a chart.

YOU WILL NEED

TO MAKE A PICTURE 20 CM/8 IN SQUARE
14-count Zweigart Aida fabric in 304,
30 cm/12 in square
DMC Stranded Cotton, 1 skein in each of
the following colours: 3816 pale green,
500 dark green, 647 pale grey,
414 mid grey, 535 dark grey,
3799 charcoal grey, 3721 rust,
921 orange, 783 golden yellow
and 742 yellow
masking tape
embroidery hoop, optional
size 24 tapestry needle
mounting board, 20 cm/8 in square
button thread
darning needle
picture frame

MAKING UP

1 Centring the design and following the weave of the Aida, make a line of tacking (basting) stitches around the picture, just larger than the mounting board. Place the cross stitch face down on the work surface and place the mounting board on top.

2 Centre the mounting board on the back of the embroidery and align the tacking (basting) stitches with the edges. Fold the Aida around the edges and turn the board over. Using button thread and a darning needle, lace together two opposite edges.

STITCHING

Fold the Aida in half in each direction to establish the centre and tack (baste) along the folds. Bind the edges of the Aida with masking tape to prevent fraying. Fit the fabric into the embroidery hoop, if used.

Using two strands of cotton over one square of Aida, cross-stitch the design from the chart. Then work the glazing bars on the windows and the detail on the door in back stitch using a single strand of 500. Work the horizontal bars on the railings, steps and the ornamental ironwork at the windows in the same way using 3799.

When the cross stitch is completed take it out of the hoop and trim off the masking tape. Pin out and press.

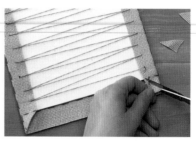

3 Trim a triangle of fabric from the corners. Check that the tacking (basting) stitches are straight, then lace together the remaining opposite edges. Place in the picture frame.

TIN CAN TREASURE

Tie a cross stitch "label" around an empty tin can and make a very pretty container for pencils or flowers. Put dried flowers straight in or put fresh flowers in a jar of water inside the can. You could adapt the idea to fit cans of all sizes.

YOU WILL NEED

14-count Charles Craft Aida in Blue Ridge, approximately 10 cm/4 in larger in each direction than the label on the can
Anchor Stranded Cotton, 1 skein in each of the following colours: 279 lime green, 243 bright green, 281 khaki green, 862 dark green, 309 rust, 20 crimson and 905 dark brown
large, clean can
masking tape
size 24 tapestry needle
fusible non-woven interlining
1.50 m/1½ yd seam binding, in a toning colour
sewing thread, to match binding

STITCHING

Fold the Aida in half in each direction to establish the centre and tack (baste) along the folds. Bind the edges of the Aida with masking tape to prevent fraying.

Starting in the centre and using two strands of cotton over one square of Aida, stitch the design from the chart.

When the cross stitch is completed remove the masking tape. Pin out and press.

MAKING UP

1 Using the can label as a guide, cut the Aida to fit around the can, covering the metal lip at the top and bottom. Cut a piece of non-woven interlining to the same size and iron it to the wrong side of the Aida. Fold the seam binding in half lengthways and press the fold. Cut a length to fit around the Aida fabric then cut the remaining binding into four equal lengths for ties. Machine-stitch along the ties lengthways, as folded.

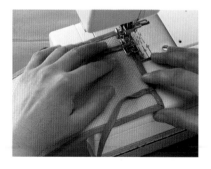

2 Pin and tack (baste) the long piece of seam binding around the Aida to enclose the raw edge, making a tuck at each corner and joining the ends of the binding underneath one of these tucks. On the right side, about 2.5 cm/1 in along one short edge, slip the end of one tie underneath the seam binding. Pin in place. Repeat with the remaining three ties. (The ties face away from the closing so that the two bound edges will butt up closely when fastened.)

3 With the right side facing, machine-stitch around the Aida close to the edge of the seam binding, pulling the pins out as you go. Tie the "label" around the can, fastening the ties in bows.

SEASON'S GREETINGS

Handmade Christmas cards are a labour of love to stitch but they're sure to be treasured by the recipients and may well find a place among the annual decorations.

YOU WILL NEED

FOR THE CHERUB DESIGN
18-count Aida fabric in white,
20 cm x 15 cm/8 in x 6 in
DMC Stranded Cotton, 1 skein in each of
the following colours: 3779 pink, 783
yellow, 3766 blue, 349 red and 905 green
DMC Metallisé, 1 skein each of
Argent and Or
15 cm x 20 cm/6 in x 8 in white
card (cardboard)

FOR THE GARLAND DESIGN
22-count Aida fabric in white,
16 cm/6¼ in square
DMC Stranded Cotton, 1 skein in each of
the following colours: 349 red, 905 green,
500 pine, 834 yellow and 3031 brown
DMC Metallisé, 1 skein each of
Argent and Or
22 cm x 11 cm/8½ in x 4¼ in white
card (cardboard)

FOR BOTH DESIGNS
masking tape
size 24 tapestry needle
double-sided adhesive tape

MAKING UP

1 Score lightly the card (cardboard) for the cherub design across the centre to measure 15 cm x 10 cm/6 in x 4 in and fold. Fold the card (cardboard) for the garland design in the same way to measure 11 cm/4¼ in square. Trim the Aida fabric to be slightly smaller than the front of the card (cardboard). Pulling out one thread at a time, carefully fray the edge of the Aida fabric to create a border.

2 Stick lengths of double-sided adhesive tape close together in parallel lines all over the wrong side of the embroidery, except the frayed edge. Peel off the protective backing.

3 Position the embroidery on the card (cardboard). Lower it into place and, with your hand, press it down working from the centre outwards. Both designs will fit into a size C6 envelope.

STITCHING

Fold the Aida fabric in half in each direction to establish the centre and tack (baste) along these folds. Bind the edges of the Aida with masking tape to prevent fraying.

Starting in the centre and using two strands of cotton over one square of Aida, cross-stitch the design following the chart. When using Metallisé, double one strand in the needle and knot the end. Then, on the cherub design, use two strands of cotton to back-stitch the eyes with 3766, mouths with 349, flower stems with 905 and a border with Or. On the garland, use 3031 to back-stitch the ends of the hips. When the stitching is completed remove the masking tape and press.

PISCINE PINCUSHION

A flat fish makes an unusual pincushion, although the pins that form the fins and tail are purely decorative. This project uses cross stitch on canvas, needlepoint style, to make an all-over stitched fabric.

YOU WILL NEED

14-count single-mesh canvas, 25 cm/10 in square
Paterna Persian Yarn, 1 skein in each of the following colours: 585 blue, 583 turquoise, 117 purple, 923 pink and 843 coral
waterproof felt-tipped pen
masking tape
size 22 tapestry needle
paper
backing fabric, 25 cm/10 in square
matching sewing thread
stuffing
long dressmaker's pins

STITCHING

Mark the centre thread on the canvas horizontally and vertically with a waterproof felt-tipped pen. Bind the raw edges with masking tape.

Starting in the centre and using one strand of Persian Yarn over one thread of canvas, stitch the design following the chart.

2 Place the finished work over a piece of paper and use a needle to pierce around the edge of the design, producing a perforated outline on the paper. Cut out a paper template along the outline.

MAKING UP

1 When the cross stitch is completed, back-stitch around the edge with 585 to give a smooth outline. Damp press on the right side.

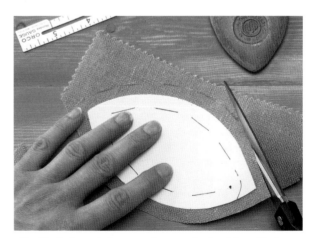

3 Tack (baste) the template to the backing fabric and cut out the fish shape, leaving a 1 cm/⅜ in seam allowance.

4 Leaving the same seam allowance, cut out the cross stitch fish.

5 Right sides together, stitch the backing fabric to the cross stitch, leaving an opening on one side. Remove the paper template and turn the fish through to the right side.

6 Fill the fish shape with stuffing.

7 Slip-stitch the opening closed. Make a tail and fins by pushing long pins into the seam.

GAME OF TAG

Making a luggage-label-style tag for your embroidery scissors means you can find them quickly. It's also a nice single-colour cross stitch exercise, with white stitched around the initial to reverse it out of a dark background.

YOU WILL NEED
18-count Aida in navy, 15 cm x 10 cm/6 in x 4 in
Anchor Nordin, 1 skein of white
masking tape
size 24 tapestry needle
luggage label
dressmaker's chalk
small piece of spotted fabric
navy sewing thread
eyelet and eyelet tool
hairgrip (bobby pin)

MAKING UP

1 Use a luggage label to draw an outline on the Aida fabric with dressmaker's chalk, centring the embroidery in the rectangular part of the label. Make 1 cm/⅜ in seam allowances all round. Draw the same shape on the spotted fabric. Right sides together, stitch together these two shapes, leaving an opening in one side. Trim and turn through to the right side.

STITCHING
Place your chosen charted initial inside the charted frame by photocopying the chart for the initial and that for the frame and pasting one onto the other. The central guidelines on both charts should match up. Any blank background squares can be filled in.

Fold the Aida in half in each direction to establish the centre and tack (baste) along the folds. Bind the edges with masking tape to prevent fraying.

Starting in the centre and using a single strand of Nordin over one square of Aida, stitch the design from the chart. When the cross stitch is completed remove the masking tape and tacking (basting) threads.

2 Slip-stitch the opening closed. Top-stitch around the tag on the right side. ▶

3 Mark the position of the eyelet. Insert the eyelet, following the manufacturer's instructions.

4 To make the rouleau, cut a 4 cm/1½ in wide bias strip from the spotted fabric. Fold it in half lengthways and machine-stitch 1 cm/⅜ in from the edge. Trim the seam.

5 Trim one end of the strip diagonally and insert a hairgrip (bobby pin) in the point of the diagonal. Using the hairgrip (bobby pin) as an aid, turn the rouleau through to the right side. Slip the rouleau through the eyelet of the tag, knot the ends and then knot it through the handle of the scissors.

OFF THE PEG

Simple check tea towels and a lively, leafy tulip design combine to make an old-fashioned peg bag that's too pretty to leave out in the rain. Even if you don't have a washing line, you could probably find a use for this handy bag.

YOU WILL NEED

2 red and white check tea towels, each approximately 50 cm x 76 cm/20 in x 30 in

DMC Stranded Cotton, 6 skeins of 3808 green and 2 skeins of 304 red

size 22 tapestry needle

wooden coat hanger, 40 cm/16 in wide

hacksaw

sandpaper

water-soluble embroidery marking pen

white sewing thread

STITCHING

Tack (baste) a central guideline down the length of each tea towel. To mark the centre of each cross stitch design, tack (baste) a line across each towel 22 cm/8½ in from the top edge. Treating the checks of the tea towel as an 8-count fabric – that is, 8 stitches to 2.5 cm/1 in – use six strands of cotton to stitch the design from chart 1 at the top of one tea towel and the design from chart 2 at the top of the second.

MAKING UP

1 Mark 2.5 cm/1 in from each end of the coat hanger. Saw off each end so that the coat hanger measures 35 cm/14 in. Sand the ends.

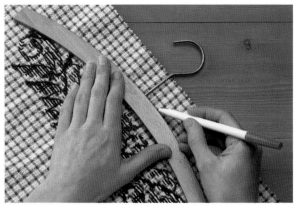

2 Measure 6 cm/2½ in above cross stitch design 1 and cut across the tea towel. Cut the opposite end to make a panel 56 cm/22 in long. On the wrong side, position the coat hanger above the design and draw along the top edge with a water-soluble marking pen. Measure and mark the position of the side seams, 37 cm/14½ in apart.

▶

3 Lay out cross stitch design 2, right side facing and the design upside down. Right sides together, position design 1, with its design the right way up, on design 2, the top of the panel about 3 cm/1¼ in from the top edge of the design 2 tea towel. Check that the centre guidelines match. Tack (baste) around the curved edge and down the side seams only.

4 Machine-stitch along the tacked (basted) outline, leaving a central 1 cm/⅜ in opening at the top for the coat hanger hook. Reinforce the seam at the opening with zigzag stitching. Trim the seam, clip notches along the curved edge and turn right side out.

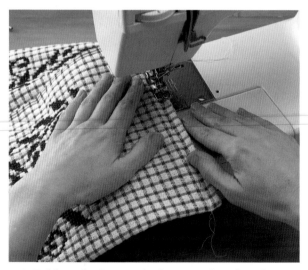

5 Fit the coat hanger inside. Fold the uncut bottom edge 10 cm (4 in) so that it overlaps the cut edge. Tack (baste) and slip-stitch to close the hem.

6 Fold up the hemmed edge to make a bag, leaving approximately 2.5 cm/1 in below each cross stitch design. Pin and tack (baste) the side seams. Machine a double row of stitching through all thicknesses, reinforcing the seams at the bag opening.

HEART APRON

The handsome crest on this stout cotton apron was inspired by Scandinavian wedding shirts.
If you don't like the idea of subjecting your needlework to rough treatment, use the design on a
cushion or a small curtain.

YOU WILL NEED

1 m/40 in of 30-count evenweave, off-white, heavy (Homespun)
cotton fabric, at least 70 cm/27½ in wide
Anchor Nordin, 3 skeins of 47 red
apron, with bib
large embroidery hoop
size 24 tapestry needle
approximately 1 m/40 in matching bias binding
matching sewing thread
1.50 m/1½ yd narrow carpet webbing

MAKING UP

1 Allowing 1 cm/⅜ in turnings on the curved edges and 2.5 cm/1 in turnings on all other edges, cut out the apron. Cut two lengths of bias binding to fit the curved edges. Open out one edge of each length of binding and press to a curve.

STITCHING

Using the apron as a pattern, fold the fabric in half length-ways and mark the outline of the apron on both sides of the fold. Don't cut it out at this stage. The design will measure approximately 23 cm x 17 cm/9 in x 6¾ in. Position the design by tacking (basting) along the fold and then hori-zontally across it where the centre of the design is to be. Fit the fabric into the embroidery hoop.

Starting in the centre and using a single strand of Nordin over two threads of fabric, stitch the design from the chart. When the cross stitch is completed remove the fabric from the embroidery hoop and press.

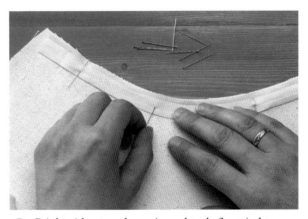

2 Right sides together, pin and tack (baste) the opened fold of each length of bias binding along the seam line of each curve. Machine-stitch, trim and clip the curved edge of the fabric only, then turn the binding to the wrong side. ▶

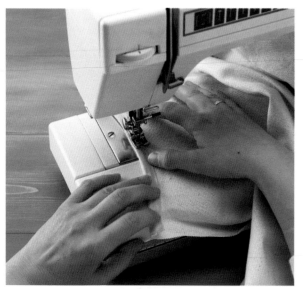

3 Tack (baste) close to the folded edge of the bias
binding and machine-stitch.

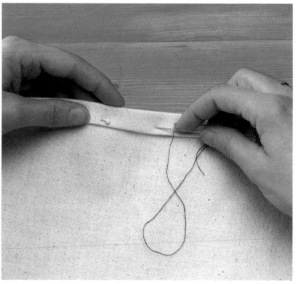

4 Make double hems top and bottom by folding
1 cm/⅜ in in to the wrong side, followed by
1.5 cm/⅝ in. Press and tack. Do the same with the
side hems, opening out the bottom corners and trimming away a small triangle of excess fabric.

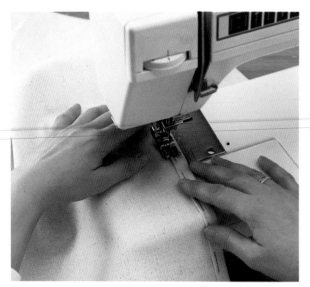

5 Machine-stitch the top, bottom and side hems
close to the folded edge.

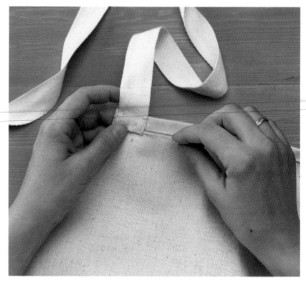

6 Cut the webbing for the neck, turn in the ends
and sew in place on the wrong side. Cut the
remaining webbing in half and sew to each side in
the same way. Trim the ends diagonally.

SHELF LIFE

Decorate a plain shelf with an edging of curly leaves in a Deco combination of green and orange.
As well as being used as a repeat pattern, the leaves could be scattered as a random design
on a tablecloth or a cushion.

YOU WILL NEED

Zweigart white linen band 7312, 8 cm/3 in wide and approximately
10 cm/4 in longer than the shelf
DMC Stranded Cotton in the following colours: 911 emerald
green, 907 bright green, 986 dark green, 470 olive green, 918
rust, 900 orange and 3821 yellow
masking tape
size 24 tapestry needle
white sewing thread
double-sided adhesive tape

MAKING UP

1 Remove the masking tape from the ends of the band and oversew the edges.

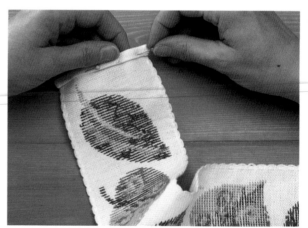

2 Pin a small double hem on each end of the band and slip-stitch. Stick a length of double-sided adhesive tape along the front edge of the shelf, remove the protective backing and press the band into position. Alternatively, use decorative pins or tacks to secure the edging.

STITCHING

Bind the ends of the linen band with masking tape to pre-vent fraying. Fold the band in half widthways to establish the centre and tack (baste) along this fold to make a verti-cal guideline. Count the threads across the depth of the band to establish the centre horizontally and tack (baste) this guideline.

When stitching a repeat, it is important to begin in the centre. Centring the repeats will leave an equal amount of part-repeat at each end. There are subtle differences between the motifs within this repeat – the two heart-shaped leaves lie in the same direction but their colours are reversed, while the oval leaves alternate in direction. Starting in the centre and using three strands of cotton over two strands of linen, stitch the design from the chart.

PLACE SETTING

Chickens and flowers are popular cross stitch motifs throughout Europe and are particularly appropriate for the kitchen. This design is made from a traditional tea towel and the woven border was the starting point for the colour scheme.

YOU WILL NEED

TO MAKE TWO PLACEMATS, EACH 50 CM X 30 CM/20 IN X 12 IN

linen tea towel, approximately 50 cm x 75 cm/20 in x 30 in
DMC Flower Thread, 4 skeins of 2823 navy and 2 skeins of 2321 red
masking tape
size 24 tapestry needle
embroidery hoop
matching sewing thread

STITCHING

Cut the tea towel in half widthways. Take one piece and fold it in half in each direction to establish the centre. Tack (baste) along the two folds. Bind the raw edge with masking tape to prevent fraying.

Using a single strand of Flower Thread, experiment to see how many threads need to be covered to make cross stitches to a count of 13 or 14 to 2.5 cm/1 in. Our fabric was not evenweave and so each stitch was worked over three threads across and two threads down. Fit the linen into the embroidery hoop. Starting in the centre, stitch the design from the chart. Use 2321 to work French knots for the eyes.

When the cross stitch is completed take the fabric out of the embroidery hoop. Pin out and press.

MAKING UP

1 Trim the existing top or bottom hem. Fold under and press a turning along the top and bottom edges to make a placemat 30 cm/12 in deep.

2 Trim the hem allowances to 1.5 cm/⅝ in and turn under the raw edge to make a narrow double hem. Machine-stitch close to the edge. Make the second placemat in the same way.

CAKE RIBBON

Dress up your cake with a large pink bow. The trompe l'oeil effect would make even a plain cake look celebratory. The linen band is durable and washable, so it's a practical idea that could become a family teatime favourite.

YOU WILL NEED

Zweigart white linen band 7273, 12 cm/
4¾ in deep (or a 7312 band, 8 cm/3 in
deep, according to the depth of your cake)
and 10 cm/4 in longer than the
circumference of the cake tin
DMC Stranded Cotton, 2 skeins each of
604 pale pink and 3806 mid pink, 1 skein
each of 3804 fuchsia and 3802 wine
masking tape
size 24 tapestry needle
white sewing thread
3 small buttons

STITCHING

Bind the ends of the linen band with masking tape to prevent fraying. Fold the band in half width-ways to establish the centre and tack (baste) along this fold to make a vertical guideline. Count the threads across the depth of the band to establish the centre horizontally and tack (baste) this guideline.

Starting in the centre and using three strands of cotton over two threads of linen, stitch the design from the chart. When the cross stitch is completed remove the masking tape and press the band.

MAKING UP

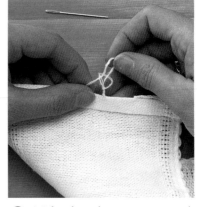

1 Adjust the length of the band to fit the cake tin. Using sewing thread or linen frayed from the band, stitch a small double hem at each end.

2 Make three loops on one end of the band, either by work-ing buttonhole stitch over a bar of thread or, as here, making a chain with the thread.

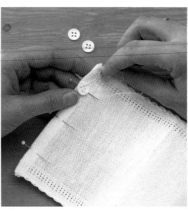

3 Sew three buttons on the other end of the band to correspond with the loops.

LEAFY PORTFOLIO

Cross-stitch a fern in the style of a botanical print and then use it to cover a portfolio. This could be used to hold sketches, paintings, letters or recipes. The bookbinding skills needed to make the portfolio are fairly basic and so are the materials and equipment.

YOU WILL NEED

TO MAKE A PORTFOLIO TO FIT SIZE A4 PAPER
28-count Zweigart Quaker Cloth,
60 cm x 40 cm/24 in x 15¾ in
DMC Stranded Cotton, 1 skein in each of
the following colours: 472 pale green, 907
yellow-green, 906 bright green, 320 blue-
green, 904 dark green, 936 olive green,
3790 light brown and 3021 dark brown
masking tape
large embroidery hoop
size 24 tapestry needle
white mounting board, a size A1 sheet
craft knife and cutting board
metal rule and set square
artist's quality PVA adhesive (white glue)
5 cm/2 in wide brown bookbinding tape
50 cm/20 in cream seam binding tape
knife with rounded blade
Canson paper, a half imperial sheet

STITCHING

Bind the edges of the fabric with masking tape to prevent fraying. Fold the fabric in half widthways to establish the position of the spine. 13 cm/ 5 in to the right of this fold tack (baste) a vertical guideline for positioning the cross stitch design. Halfway down tack (baste) a horizontal guideline to establish the centre of the design. Fit the fabric into the embroidery hoop.

Starting in the centre and using two strands of cotton over two threads of fabric, stitch the design following the chart.

When the cross stitch is completed take it out of the embroidery hoop and press.

MAKING UP

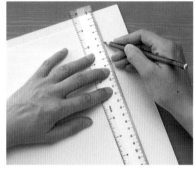

1 Using a craft knife and cutting mat, cut two pieces of mounting board 23 cm x 32 cm/9 in x 12½ in. With right sides facing and lining up the grain of the fabric with the edge of the board, centre the cross stitch design on one piece of board for the front.

2 Turn over and line up the second piece of board for the back, leaving a space of 2.5 cm/ 1 in for the spine. Trim the fabric to within 2.5 cm/1 in of the outer edge of the boards.

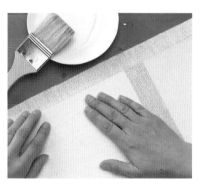

3 Spread PVA (white glue) generously over the face of one board and press on the fabric. Repeat with the other board. Turn over and smooth out any air bubbles. Leave to dry.

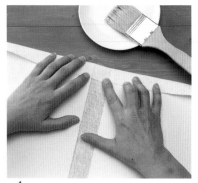

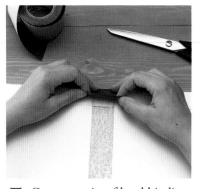

4 Cut across each outside corner of the fabric at 45 degrees. Turn the fabric over the boards, at the same time turning it in at the spine. Stick down with PVA (white glue). Press firmly and leave to dry.

5 Cut one strip of bookbinding tape 5 cm/2 in longer than the spine and one piece 1 cm/ ⅜ in shorter than the spine. Peel off the backing and stick the longer tape along the outside spine, leaving equal ends free top and bottom. Fold the ends in and press to stick.

6 Stick the shorter strip of bookbinding tape along the inside spine, leaving an equal margin top and bottom.

7 Cut four 10 cm/4 in lengths of bookbinding tape. Peel off the backing, centre the tape on the outside of a corner at 45 degrees, wrap it around the corner and press to stick. Repeat for the other three corners.

8 Mark and cut a slot slightly wider than the seam binding tape 1 cm/⅜ in from the outer edge centrally on the outside of the back and front. Cut the tape into two equal lengths. Use a rounded knife blade to push the end of one tape through the slot from outside to inside. Glue the tape inside securely, with the end facing away from the edge. Repeat with the second tape.

9 Cut two inside cover papers from the Canson paper, slightly smaller than the folder. Stick one inside each cover.

CURTAIN CALL

Grapes and vines have featured in cross stitch for centuries, both as symbols of plenty and for their decorative qualities. Here, a large border pattern runs along a length of coarsely woven linen to make a small, semi-sheer curtain.
The colouring is kept creamy and quiet.

YOU WILL NEED

TO MAKE A CURTAIN 112 CM x 60 CM/44 IN x 24 IN
20-count off-white evenweave linen, 1.30 m x 80 cm/51 in x 31½ in
DMC Stranded Cotton, 9 skeins of 644 grey-green and 6 skeins of
822 cream
matching sewing thread
large embroidery hoop
size 22 or 24 tapestry needle
curtain clips

STITCHING

Fold the linen in half in each direction to establish the centre and tack (baste) along the folds. Oversew by hand or machine zigzag the edges of the linen to prevent fraying.

Fit the fabric into the embroidery hoop. Starting in the centre of the fabric and using three strands of cotton over three threads of linen, stitch the design from the chart. Then, starting at the arrowheads, stitch the repeat indicated by broken lines, completing the tip of the leaf. When the cross stitch is completed take the linen out of the frame and press.

MAKING UP

1 Tack (baste) the finished size of the curtain on the linen, following the grain of the fabric. Trim carefully along the grain, leaving a hem allowance of 6 cm/2½ in on each side.

2 Fold the outer 3 cm/1¼ in of the hem allowance to the wrong side and press along the fold. Fold these two layers again to make a 3 cm/1¼ in double hem and press carefully along the straight grain. ▶

3 Wrong side facing, open out the hem at one corner and fold the linen diagonally to make a triangle. The tacked (basted) corner should just show in the centre of the folded edge.

4 Press, then trim the triangle 4 cm/1½ in from the folded edge. Repeat with the other three corners.

5 Refold the hem to make neat mitred corners, then pin and tack (baste) the hem and corners.

6 Machine-stitch close to the edge of the hem. Slip-stitch closed the diagonal folds of the mitred corners. Attach clips to hang the curtain from a pole or rod.

PERSONALIZED TABLE LINEN

Stitched in the corner of a linen table napkin, a large initial looks very flamboyant. Designed on the diagonal, it's no more difficult to stitch than a conventional letter and could be worked on any square item from a handkerchief to a bedspread.

YOU WILL NEED

TO MAKE A TABLE NAPKIN 43 CM /17 IN SQUARE
coloured linen, 45 cm/17¾ in square
DMC Flower Thread, 1 skein in white
sewing thread, to match linen
small embroidery hoop
size 24 tapestry needle

MAKING UP

1 Fold and press the 1 cm/⅜ in single hem along the tacked (basted) guideline. Open out the hem at each corner, turn in and press a triangle of fabric to touch the tacked (basted) corner. Refold the hem and press the resulting mitred corner.

STITCHING

With matching thread, lightly zigzag around the edges of the linen to prevent fraying. Tack (baste) a line 1 cm/⅜ in from the edges which will be the fold of a small single hem. Allowing for the hem, tack (baste) two intersecting guidelines in the corner of the napkin to mark the centre of the initial to be stitched. The size of the initial will be determined by the size of stitch produced by the fabric count. This linen was not evenweave and so the stitches were worked over two threads down and three threads across to produce 15 stitches to 2.5 cm/1 in. This letter measures approximately 6.5 cm x 5.5 cm/2½ in x 2¼ in.

Fit the fabric into the embroidery hoop. Starting in the centre and using a single strand of Flower Thread, stitch the design from the chart. When the cross stitch is completed take it out of the embroidery hoop and press.

2 Tack (baste) the hem, then closely machine-, zigzag- or satin-stitch along the edge.

FRUIT FLAVOURS

A pot of homemade jam or jelly topped with a hand-embroidered cover to match would transform a homely gift into a very special one. The stitched fruit designs could also be framed as a set of small pictures.

YOU WILL NEED

FOR EACH COVER

32-count cream linen, 20 cm/8 in square

Anchor Stranded Cotton, 1 skein in each of the following colours:

FOR THE REDCURRANTS

212 dark green, 267 mid green, 215 blue-green, 280 yellow-green, 39 pink-red, 29 scarlet, 28 pink, 333 orange and 905 brown

FOR THE CHERRIES

683 dark green, 216 mid green, 214 light green, 22 wine, 1005 crimson, 77 pink, 382 dark brown and 898 light brown

FOR THE STRAWBERRIES

862 dark green, 266 olive green, 243 bright green, 9046 bright red, 13 dull red, 11 deep pink and 907 ochre

masking tape

small embroidery hoop

size 24 or 26 tapestry needle

elastic bands

natural raffia or string

MAKING UP

1 Place the linen over a jam pot and measure the drop of the corners to half the depth of the pot. Trim the linen to this size.

2 Pull a thread in the linen to mark the point up to which the linen can be frayed and still leave enough fabric to tie at the neck of the pot.

STITCHING

Fold the linen in half in each direction to find the centre and tack (baste) along the folds. Bind the edges with masking tape and fit into the embroidery hoop.

Starting in the centre and using two strands of cotton over two threads of linen, cross-stitch the design from the charts. Then work the back stitch details using two strands of cotton. On the redcurrants use 267 for the stems and the base of the currants. On the cherries use 216 for the leaf stems and 683 for the fruit stems. On the strawberries use 907 for the seeds and 266 for the stems. Take the stitching out of the hoop and remove the masking tape. Pin out and press.

3 Fray the edge of the linen by pulling out one thread at a time. Pot and seal the jam. Place the cover on the jam pot, secured with an elastic band covered with raffia or string.

TRADITIONAL SAMPLER

With its soft, faded colouring and deliberately archaic style, this sampler could pass for an antique. By including your own family's initials and the present date, you could make it into an heirloom for the future.

YOU WILL NEED

TO MAKE A SAMPLER WITH A STITCHED AREA 23.5 CM X 28.5 CM/9¼ IN X 11¼ IN 32-count raw linen, approximately 38 cm x 46 cm/15 in x 18 in
Anchor Stranded Cotton, 1 skein in each of the following colours: 874 yellow, 858 sage, 217 green, 860 khaki, 875 acqua, 840 spruce, 850 teal, 1033 blue, 1016 rose, 895 coral, 897 wine, 889 umber, 382 dark brown and 926 cream
masking tape
straight-sided embroidery frame
size 24 or 26 tapestry needle
mounting board
heavyweight non-woven interlining
double-sided adhesive tape
long dressmaker's pins
button thread
picture frame

STITCHING

Fold the linen in half in each direction to establish the centre and tack (baste) along the folds. Bind the edges of the linen with masking tape. Mount the linen on the frame.

Starting in the centre and using two strands of cotton over two threads of linen, stitch the design from the chart.

When the cross stitch is completed take the sampler out of the frame and remove the masking tape. Pin out and press.

MAKING UP

1 Decide on the depth of border around the stitched area and cut the mounting board to the appropriate size. Cut the interlining to the same size. Stick several lengths of double-sided adhesive tape to the board, peel off the protective backing and press the interlining onto the tape.

2 Lay the wrong side of the sampler on the padded board. Position the design, fold the linen around the edges of the board and turn the board over. Aligning the grain of the linen with the edges of the board and pushing the pins into the board, pin two opposite sides.

3 When the linen is evenly taut, use button thread to lace together the opposite edges of the linen.

4 Making neat, flat folds at the corners, pin and lace together the second pair of opposite sides in the same way. Fit the sampler in the picture frame.

LIGHT WORK

Embroidery on a lampshade creates two effects – a coloured design by daylight and a silhouette by lamplight. The stitched fabric is simply fitted over an existing shade. Choose bright-coloured threads and the moths will become butterflies.

YOU WILL NEED

28-count Zweigart Annabelle cotton fabric,
76 cm/30 in square
DMC Stranded Cotton, 1 skein in each of
the following colours: 300 rust, 435
cinnamon, 3046 corn, 3823 cream,
3822 yellow, 833 ochre, 928 pale grey,
3022 mid grey, 3021 dark brown and
3787 grey-brown
coolie-style lampshade,
38 cm/15 in diameter
76 cm/30 in square of brown paper
pencil
water-soluble embroidery marking pen
embroidery hoop
size 24 tapestry needle
double-sided adhesive tape
bias binding, optional

MAKING UP

1 Drape the fabric around the lampshade to check that the back seam and edges match up. Trim, leaving a 1.5 cm/⅝ in seam allowance all round. Fold under the back seam allowances and press. Stick double-sided tape around the inside of the lampshade at the top and bottom. Stick a length on the outside down the back seam.

2 Remove the protective backing paper, butt the edges of the fabric at the back seam and press onto the tape.

3 Turn under the raw edges and stick them securely to the inside of the frame, snipping the top edge to fit around the lamp support. The raw edges can be covered with bias binding if required. Slip-stitch the back seam to complete.

PREPARATION AND STITCHING

Roll the shade across the paper to make a pattern, beginning at the side seam and rolling until the side seam touches the paper again. Mark the curved bottom edge in pencil as you go. Repeat along the top edge, then draw two straight lines for the back seam. Cut out the pattern and check the fit on the shade.

Lay the pattern on the fabric and trace it using the water-soluble embroidery marking pen. Tack (baste) along the lines. Position the moths,

remembering that the angle of the motifs will depend on the grain of the fabric.

Fit the fabric into the embroidery hoop. Starting in the centre of a motif and using two strands of cotton over two threads of fabric, stitch the design from the chart. Work the back stitch details using one strand of cotton in the shade indicated.

When the cross stitch is completed take the fabric out of the embroidery hoop. Pin out and press.

ALL SET FOR BED

Hand-stitched linen is an impossible luxury unless you make your own.
This small, decorative cushion could just as easily be a full-sized pillow.
The matching flower head on the sheet is a detail from the design.

YOU WILL NEED

TO MAKE A SINGLE SHEET 254 CM X 178 CM/
100 IN X 70 IN AND A CUSHION COVER TO FIT
A 30 CM X 50 CM/12 IN X 19½ IN CUSHION
3.30 m/3¾ yd of 178 cm/70 in wide white
cotton sheeting fabric
Anchor Stranded Cotton, 1 skein in each
of the following colours: 117 pale blue,
176 mid blue and 941 dark blue
10-count waste canvas, 32 cm x 25 cm/
12½ in x 10 in and another piece 10 cm/
4 in square
size 5 crewel needle
white sewing thread
plastic water spray
tweezers

PREPARATION AND STITCHING

SHEET

Cut out a rectangle of cotton fabric the width of the fabric x 264 cm/ 104 in long. Hem the top edge of the sheet by making a 1 cm/⅜ in turning, followed by a 5 cm/2 in turning, then satin-stitch. Along the bottom edge make a 1 cm/⅜ in turning, followed by a 3 cm/1¼ in turning and machine-stitch. Leave the selvedges along the sides unhemmed.

Fold the sheet in half lengthways and measure 15 cm/6 in along this fold from the top edge to establish the centre of the flower head motif. Tack (baste) the smaller piece of waste canvas in place. Starting in the centre and using two strands of cotton, stitch the flower head from the main chart.

When the cross stitch is completed trim the waste canvas close to the stitching. Spray with water to damp the stitches and canvas. Use tweezers to pull out the waste canvas, one thread at a time.

CUSHION COVER

For the cushion front cut a piece 75 cm x 55 cm/29½ in x 21½ in. For the back cut one piece 54 x 34 cm/ 21¼ in x 13½ in and an underlap piece 16 cm x 34 cm/6½ in x 13½ in.

Fold the cushion front in half in each direction to establish the centre and tack (baste) along the folds. Zigzag-stitch the edges of the fabric to prevent them fraying. Tack (baste) the larger piece of waste canvas in position on the right side, centred on the guidelines. Starting in the centre and using two strands of cotton, stitch the design from the chart.

When the cross stitch is completed trim the waste canvas close to the stitching and remove threads as for the sheet.

MAKING UP

1 On the cushion front piece, fold and press a 1 cm/⅜ in turning to the wrong side on all edges, followed by a 5 cm/2 in turning to make a double hem.

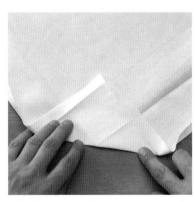

2 Open out these turnings and fold each corner diagonally to the wrong side, lining up the inner folds to make a right angle. Press the diagonal folds. ▶

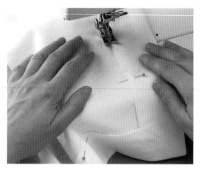

3 Open out, turn over and refold, cut edges together, so that the two halves of each pressed diagonal fold can be pinned, tacked (basted) and machine-stitched to form a seam. Trim the seam allowance, as shown, and press open. Turn through to the right side, refolding to complete the mitred corners of the border.

4 Hem one short edge of the back piece by making a 5 mm/¼ in turning, followed by a 1.5 cm/⅝ in turning, then machine-stitch. Repeat along one long edge of the underlap piece. Wrong sides together, slip the three raw edges of the underlap underneath the front cover borders. Pin and tack (baste).

5 Zigzag-stitch through all the layers along the unhemmed long edge of the underlap piece.

6 With right sides outward and hemmed edge at the same end as the underlap, pin and tack (baste) the three raw edges of the back piece underneath the three unstitched edges of the border. Zigzag-stitch through all layers along these three sides. On the front, cover the zigzag stitching with a line of close zigzag or satin stitch.

SILK THROW

This is an informal arrangement of motifs and scraps of border repeats from Eastern Europe and Asia. They're scattered over a length of raw silk to make a throw with a colourful fringe made from the same threads as the cross stitch.

YOU WILL NEED

TO MAKE A THROW 107 CM X 81 CM/
42 IN X 32 IN
26-count silk matka, approximately
117 cm x 90 cm/46 in x 36 in
the same amount of contrast lining fabric
DMC Stranded Cotton, in the following
colours: 223 pink, 3350 rose, 3721 red-
brown, 3830 rust, 3802 mulberry, 3829
ochre, 734 lime, 327 purple, 340 mauve,
3807 blue, 597 turquoise, 3810 jade, 931
blue-grey and 3768 grey-green
matching sewing thread
embroidery hoop
size 24 tapestry needle
small piece of card (cardboard)
darning needle

STITCHING

Oversew the edges of the silk to prevent fraying. Decide on the position of the motifs. Do this by photocopying the charts (enlarged to the right size – 13 stitches to 2.5 cm/ 1 in) and tacking (basting) these onto the fabric.

Setting the silk in an embroidery hoop and allowing a generous border all round, work any combination of motifs using two strands of cotton over two threads of silk. When the cross stitch is completed take it out of the embroidery hoop and press.

MAKING UP

1 Trim the edges to leave a 2 cm/¾ in seam. Right sides together, machine-stitch the stitched front and the lining together, leaving an opening of about 50 cm/20 in on one long side. Turn through to the right side.

2 With matching stranded cotton make 7 cm/2¾ in tassels. First fold in half a 14 cm/5½ in long piece of card (cardboard) and use this as a gauge. Wrap the stranded cotton around the folded card (cardboard) 20 times.

3 Insert scissors along the open edge of the card (cardboard) and cut. Then make two double wraps and cut. Use one of the longer lengths to gather together the shorter strands, by taking it underneath the fold of the shorter strands. Use the second to bind the shorter strands together, by making a flat loop alongside the doubled strands then wrapping it six times evenly around the bundle, leaving the loop free above the binding and the first end free below. ▶

4 Take the end of the binding thread through the flat loop.

5 Pull the first end of the thread (attached to the loop) so that the loop pulls the end of the binding thread down behind the binding. Trim both ends of this thread close to the tassel.

6 Trim the tassels. Knot the holding thread of each tassel just above the tassel head then thread the two ends onto a darning needle. Insert it in one of the shorter seams, draw up the tassel, turn the throw to the wrong side and back stitch in the seam allowance. Fringe both short ends in this way. Trim the corners and turn through. Slip stitch closed the opening in the last seam. Press then top stitch 1.5 cm/⅝ in from the edge.

SHIPSHAPE

Ships make perfect cross stitch designs, with their schematic patterns of sails, flags and rigging. Enhance the pattern by using gingham for the background and make a bag which can be used for socks, shoes or toys in a child's room.

YOU WILL NEED

TO MAKE A BAG 45 CM X 61 CM/17¾ IN X 24 IN

1.10 m/43 in of 90 cm/36 in wide small-check gingham

the same amount of fabric with a larger check, for the lining

Anchor Nordin, 2 skeins of 127 navy and 4 skeins of 147 blue

large embroidery hoop

size 5 crewel needle

matching sewing thread

2.20 m/2½ yd of No 6 white piping cord

large safety pin

MAKING UP

1 Place the pieces of lining fabric right sides together and, with 1.5 cm/⅝ in seam allowances throughout, machine-stitch the two long sides to make a tube. Press the seams open.

2 Do the same with the two main pieces of fabric for the bag but, 13 cm/5¼ in down from the top edge, leave a break of 3 cm/1¼ in for each side seam. Press the seams open.

PREPARATION AND STITCHING

Balancing the checks, cut out two rectangles of small-check gingham, each 48 cm x 64 cm/19 in x 25 in, for the bag. Cut the large-check fabric in the same way for the lining. Machine zigzag around the edges of one piece of small-check gingham to prevent fraying. Fold this piece in half lengthways and tack (baste) along the fold. Measure 23 cm/9 in from the bottom edge and, following a line of checks, tack (baste) a horizontal line to establish the centre. The design measures approximately 29 cm/11⅜ in deep x 27 cm/10⅝ in wide, working to a count of four cross stitches to each 3 mm/⅛ in square of the gingham. If your check fabric has a different scale this will affect the size of the design.

Fit the fabric into the embroidery hoop. Note that gingham squares are not always identical in size but working slightly inside larger ones and outside smaller ones will compensate. However, don't be too concerned about producing perfectly uniform stitches as a little irregularity adds to the charm of this type of design. If the pattern on the side of the ship is to tie in with the squares of the gingham start in this area, rather than in the centre.

Using a single strand of Nordin and working four stitches in each gingham square, stitch the design from the chart. When the cross stitch is completed take the gingham out of the embroidery hoop and press.

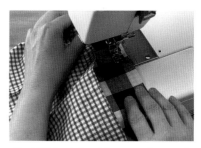

3 With right sides together and matching side seams, slip one tube inside the other. Machine-stitch the two together around the top edge. Turn through to the right side and press the top edge.

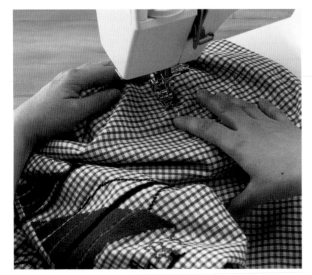

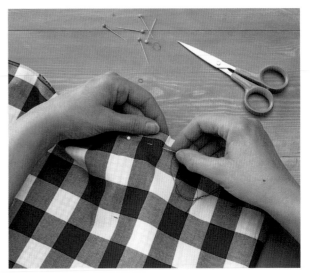

4 With the main fabric to the outside, make two parallel rows of machine stitching to form the casing for the drawstrings. Make the first one 11.5 cm/4½ in from the top edge and the second one 3 cm/1¼ in below this, either side of the opening in each outer side seam.

5 Turn the bag through to the wrong side. Machine-stitch the bottom edge through all layers of fabric (this prevents the lining pulling out when the bag is in use). Trim and oversew the edge. Turn through to the right side.

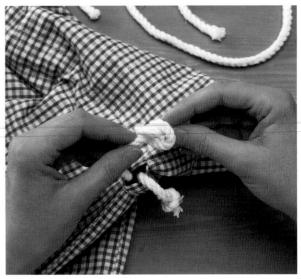

6 Cut the piping cord in half. Attach the safety pin to one end, then thread one cord through a side opening, around the casing and out at the same side opening.

7 Knot the two ends. Repeat with the second cord through the second side opening.

TURKISH CHAIR COVER

A small folding chair makes a useful bedroom chair or occasional dining chair with the addition of a cushion and slip cover. The scene stitched on the back of the slip cover has Eastern origins and includes back stitch for extra decorative detail.

YOU WILL NEED

FOR SLIP COVER AND CUSHION

approximately 1 m/1⅛ yd of 122 cm/
48 in wide striped fabric
Anchor Coton à Broder 16, 1 skein in
each of the following colours: 338 pink,
307 yellow, 341 rust, 268 green, 152 navy,
169 mid blue and 168 pale blue
12-count waste canvas, approximately
18 cm x 43 cm/7 in x 17 in
paper
large darning needle
plastic water spray
tweezers
approximately 2.20 m/2½ yd No 4 piping cord
matching sewing thread
2 pieces of 400 g/14 oz wadding (batting),
to fit the chair seat
fusible non-woven tape for hems

PREPARATION

Make paper patterns of both the chair back and seat, allowing a little extra for ease on the slip cover and for padding in the cushion.

Balancing the stripes and adding a 2.5 cm (1 in) seam allowance on all sides, use the paper patterns to cut out two rectangles of fabric for the slip cover and two for the cushion.

Cut enough 4 cm/1½ in wide bias strips to fit around the cushion and the top and sides of the slip cover. Cut four strips for ties for the cushion.

STITCHING AND MAKING UP

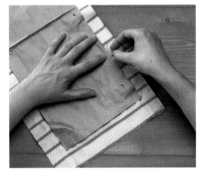

1 Leaving the paper pattern pinned to one of the slip cover pieces, tack (baste) around the edge of the pattern piece.

3 Join the bias strips with bias seams to make one continuous strip to fit around the cushion, and a second strip to fit around the top and sides of the slip cover. Fold the strips around the piping cord and stitch, using the zipper foot of the machine.

2 Pin and securely tack (baste) the waste canvas in place on the right side, trimming it to fit inside the tacked (basted) line. Fold the fabric and canvas in half widthways to establish the centre and tack (baste) this vertical guideline. Positioning it slightly above centre, fold and tack (baste) a horizontal guideline lengthways across the canvas. Starting in the centre and using a single strand of coton à broder, stitch the design from the chart. Then work the back stitch details, as shown on the chart. Trim, then spray with water to damp the stitches and waste canvas. Use tweezers to pull out the waste canvas, one thread at a time.

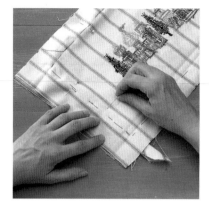

4 Right side facing and match-ing raw edges, pin and tack (baste) the piping cord around the top and sides of the slip cover. Do the same around all sides of the front of the cushion and join with a bias seam. Make up the ties by seaming them and turning them through to the right side.

5 Right sides together, pin and tack (baste) the back and front of the slip cover. Stitch close to the piping cord using the zip-per foot of the machine. Do the same with the cushion, enclosing the ties in the back seam and leaving an opening for turning through. Turn both through to the right side.

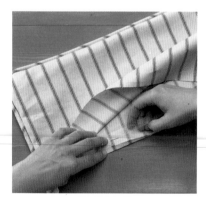

6 Hem the slip cover by mak-ing a turning along the open edges, enclosing the fusible hem tape close to the fold and then ironing to fuse the hem in place. Hand-stitch all over the two layers of wadding (batting) to make a very firm pad. Insert in the cushion cover and close the back seam.

A FINE LINE

An inexpensive waffle-weave hand towel can be turned into something very special with the addition of a little cross stitch — black on white looks particularly crisp. This border design of stylised, spiky flower heads could be used on almost any item in the linen cupboard.

YOU WILL NEED
small cotton hand towel with a plain woven border
14-count waste canvas, the size of the towel border
Anchor Coton à Broder 16, 1 skein of 403 black
small darning needle
plastic water spray
tweezers

PREPARATION

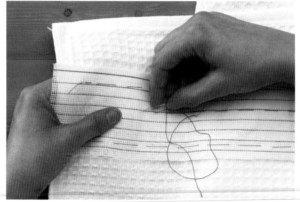

1 If necessary, pin out and damp press the end of the towel to make sure it is completely square. Trim the waste canvas to fit the border of the towel, with the contrast threads running parallel to the edge if possible. Securely tack (baste) the waste canvas in place on the right side of the border. Fold the border and canvas in half widthways to establish the centre and tack (baste) this vertical guideline, following a thread of the canvas. Using the contrast threads as an aid, count the threads of waste canvas across the depth of the border and tack (baste) a horizontal guideline along the centre of the border.

STITCHING

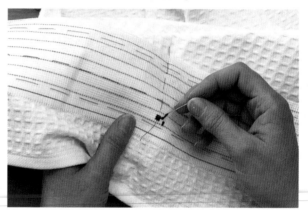

2 When stitching a repeat pattern, it is especially important to begin in the centre. Centring the repeats will leave an equal amount of part-repeat at each end. Using a single strand of coton à broder, stitch the design from the chart. The broken lines on the chart indicate the 24-stitch repeat.

When the cross stitch is completed trim the waste canvas close to the stitching. Spray with water to damp the stitches and canvas. Use tweezers to pull out the waste canvas, one thread at a time.

SHOO FLY COVER

It's a frivolous idea, but why not decorate a gauzy food cover with the very insects you are trying to keep out? Or perhaps just the more attractive-looking ones. A sheer curtain could be given the same treatment.

YOU WILL NEED
mesh food cover
Anchor Stranded Cotton, 1 skein in each of the following colours:
410 blue, 290 yellow, 335 red, 1014 rust, 281 olive green, 238
emerald green, 189 dark green, 403 black and 1 white
non-woven tear-off backing fabric
size 24 tapestry needle

PREPARATION
Decide on the position of the insects, remembering that the angle of the finished motifs will depend on the grain of the mesh fabric.

For each motif, cut a piece of non-woven tear-off backing fabric between 5 cm/2 in and 10 cm/4 in square. Pin and securely tack (baste) a square to the wrong side of the mesh.

STITCHING

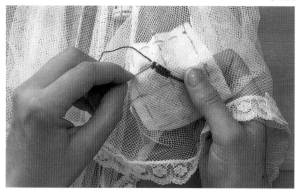

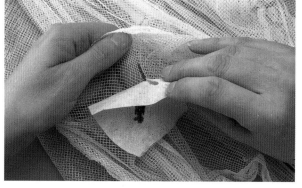

1 Using three strands of cotton and starting in the centre, stitch the design from the chart through both the mesh and the backing fabric. If starting in the usual way is difficult, leave an end of about 8 cm/ 3 in before making the first stitch and darn it in later.

2 When the cross stitch has been completed, remove the tacking (basting) threads and gently tear away the backing fabric. Now work the double running stitch using one strand of 403, except for the veins on the dragonfly's wings which are worked with two strands of 189. Double running stitch returns the needle to the starting point for darning in ends. That is, a line of running stitch is worked in one direction, and then running stitch is worked back along the same line, filling in the spaces between stitches.

DENIM ROSE

Although it was inspired by 19th-century Berlin wool work, this design of wild roses on blue denim has quite a tough, contemporary feel. Choosing different threads and fabric would change the mood completely – try wool on canvas for a Victorian look.

YOU WILL NEED

TO MAKE A CUSHION 40 CM/16 IN SQUARE

80 cm/32 in of 115 cm/54 in wide medium-weight denim

9-count waste canvas, 32 cm/12½ in square

DMC Soft Cotton, 3 skeins each of 2570 wine, 2572 dusty pink, 2326 deep pink; 2 skeins of 2309 fuchsia; 1 skein each of 2986 bottle green, 2561 dark green, 2905 mid green, 2562 grass, 2563 apple green, 2564 pale green, 2743 yellow and 2766 ochre

matching sewing thread

darning needle

plastic water spray

tweezers

contrast thread, for top stitching

cushion pad, 40 cm (16 in) square

STITCHING

Cut a 51 cm/20 in square and two rectangles 38 cm x 51 cm/15 in x 20 in from the denim. Oversew the edges of the square to prevent fraying. Tack (baste) the waste canvas securely in the centre on the right side of the denim square.

Starting in the centre and using a single strand of soft cotton and a darning needle, stitch the design from the chart. When the cross stitch is completed trim the waste canvas close to the stitching. Spray with water and pull out the waste canvas, one thread at a time.

MAKING UP

1 Along one long edge of each denim rectangle make a 1.5 cm/½ in turning, followed by a 2 cm/¾ in turning to make a double hem. Machine-stitch.

2 With right sides towards you, overlap the hemmed edges to make a 51 cm/20 in square. Tack (baste) the two rectangles together to form the cushion back.

3 With right sides together, tack (baste) the back to the front of the cushion, with the back opening running across the design from right to left. Allowing a 1.5 cm/½ in seam allowance, machine-stitch around the edge. Trim the corners and turn through to the right side.

4 Tack (baste) the edges through all layers and press. With matching thread, machine-stitch all around the cushion 4 cm/1½ in from the edge. Using this as a guideline, machine two lines of contrast top stitching. Insert the cushion pad.

MATERIALS

*There is a wide choice of fabrics suitable for cross stitch and a
tempting array of embroidery threads in every shade.*

Cross stitch can be worked on most open-weave fabrics. The fabric should also be evenweave, ie. the same number of threads to a given measurement along both the warp and weft of the fabric. The measurement used is 2.5 cm/1 in and the number of threads is referred to as the "count", so 14-count fabric has 14 threads (therefore, stitches) to 2.5 cm/1 in. As the count rises, the stitches become smaller. When the count becomes too great to work over a single thread, the stitch is worked over two threads. A 32-count fabric is worked with 16 stitches to 2.5 cm/1 in. Choose threads according to the scale of the stitch and fabric weave.

AIDA is a good fabric which comes in many colours and counts. It has a block-like weave and is firm enough to be used without a hoop. LINEN comes in a many textures and has been used through history. Linen that is made for embroidery is very easy to use. Other linens are not always evenweave and so more threads may need to be worked in one direction than the other to produce square stitches. WOVEN CHECKS provide a grid on which to work cross stitch and although the result isn't completely regular it will have a folksy charm.

SILK FABRICS are also suitable for cross stitch if you use evenweave raw silk such as noile or matka. CANVAS is a good choice if you want to fill in the background, giving an all-over effect.
WASTE CANVAS is a special kind of canvas that is used to work cross stitch on close-woven fabrics.
STRANDED COTTON is probably the best known cross stitch thread because of the huge number of colours available and the variety of thicknesses obtainable by using any number of strands from one to six. It has a slightly mercerised sheen.
FLOWER THREAD and NORDIN are fine, completely matt threads for use as a single thread.
COTON À BRODER is available in several thicknesses.
SOFT COTTON is a thicker, completely matt thread.
TAPESTRY WOOL, such as Persian Yarn, is a soft woollen thread, available in many colours.
METALLICS, as the name implies, are the shiniest threads of all.

Clockwise from top left: Aida fabric, coton à broder, canvas, waste canvas, upholstery linen, raw linen, linen, soft cotton, linen band, tapestry wool, flower thread and Nordin. In the centre, above, metallic thread, and below, stranded cotton.

EQUIPMENT

*The beauty of cross stitch is that so little equipment is
necessary that you can take it anywhere.*

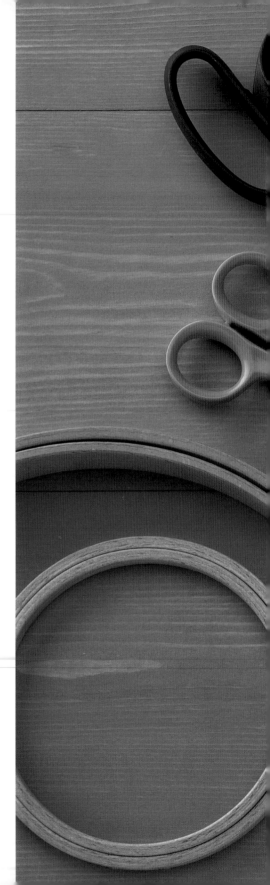

SCISSORS A large pair of scissors
is needed for cutting out fabric.
A small pair of embroidery scissors
is essential.

EMBROIDERY HOOP This is a good
idea unless you are using a firm
fabric such as Aida or one stiff-
ened with waste canvas. A hoop is
ideal if the design can be worked
in the hoop without the stitches
being crushed. Binding the two
halves with strips of muslin will
help to grip the fabric with a
minimum of pressure (see
Techniques). To put the fabric
into the hoop set the continuous
ring on a flat surface and lay the
fabric over it. With both hands,
gently and evenly press down the
adjustable ring. When the weave is
absolutely square, tighten the
screw just enough to hold the fabric. The fabric should be tensioned but not taut like a drum.
Release the screw to move the
hoop to a new area of fabric,
always centring the work. To
avoid serious creasing, take the
fabric out of the hoop whenever
it's not being worked on.

EMBROIDERY FRAME A square
frame requires more setting up but
the work can be left in it indefi-
nitely. The raw edges of the fabric
will need strengthening by binding
with tape. The top and bottom
edges, centred on the top and bottom rails of the frame, are over-
sewn to the tape attached to these
rails. The side edges of the fabric
are then laced with strong thread
to the side rails. The fabric should
be firmly and evenly tensioned
with no distortion of the weave.

NEEDLES used for cross stitch are
usually tapestry needles, with a
rounded point and an oval eye.
The rounded point is to slip
between threads without splitting
them. The eye should be large
enough to thread comfortably but
not so large that it forces apart the
threads of the fabric. Where non-
open-weave fabrics are used in this
book it is recommended that a
darning needle is used. In needle
sizing, the higher the number the
finer the needle.

MAGNIFIER This is useful when
working with fine-count fabric.

TAPE MEASURE Accurate measure-
ments are important in many of
the projects. A measuring gauge
for hems and seams is also useful.

STITCH UNPICKER This tool saves
time when removing threads.

*Clockwise from top left: embroidery
scissors, large scissors, tape measure,
embroidery frame, magnifier, measuring
gauge, stitch unpicker, needles and
embroidery hoops.*

66

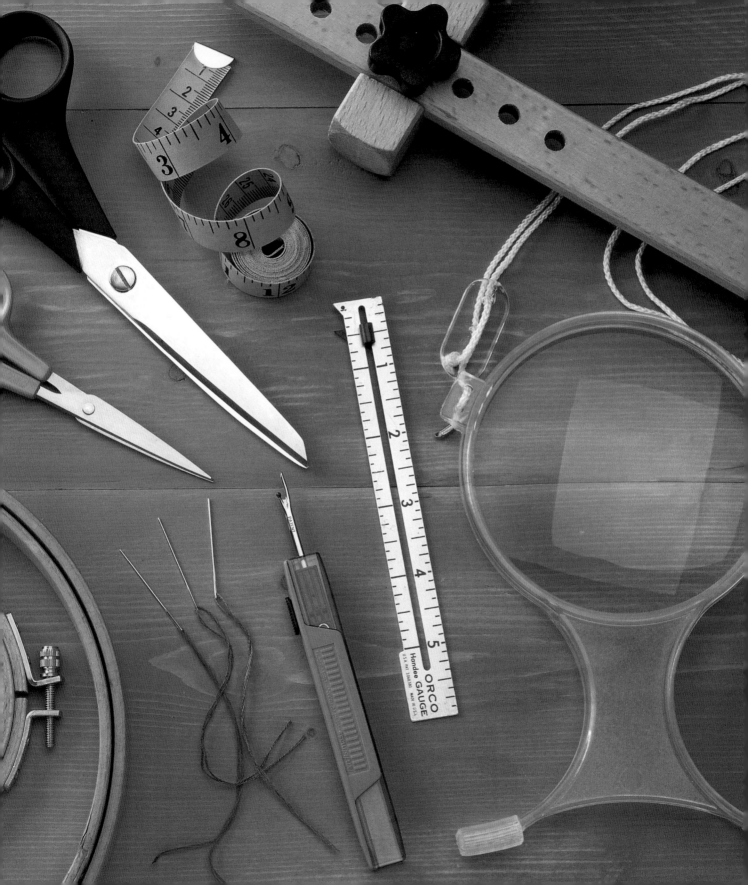

TECHNIQUES

There are a few basic techniques which will help you with your cross stitch and explain how to use the charts at the end of the book.

PREPARATION

An additional margin of fabric should be left around all projects for handling, enclosing in an embroidery hoop and limiting fraying. This varies from project to project but is usually a minimum of 5 cm (2 in) on each edge. These margins have been allowed for in the projects in this book.

PREPARING THE FABRIC
To prevent fraying during handling and stitching, the edges of the fabric should be protected, unless they are selvedges. Hemming, oversewing by hand or zigzag-stitching by machine are good methods, but the easiest and quickest way is to bind raw edges with masking tape. This can easily be pulled off or cut off afterwards.

FINDING THE CENTRE

1 Cross stitch is ususally worked from the centre of the design and so this point must be established on the fabric. Fold the fabric in half lengthways and crease along this line.

2 Tack (baste) along the creased line to mark it, following the grain of the fabric very carefully.

3 Fold the fabric widthways and tack (baste) along this line, following the grain. The intersection of the folds is the centre. These lines correspond to the lines intersecting the charts.

COVERING AN EMBROIDERY HOOP

Embroidery hoops have two rings. One is solid and the other is adjustable, with a screw fastening. The fabric is sandwiched between the rings. To protect the fabric and stitches from damage, wrap both rings with bias strips of muslin, as shown. See Equipment for instructions on fitting the fabric in the embroidery frame.

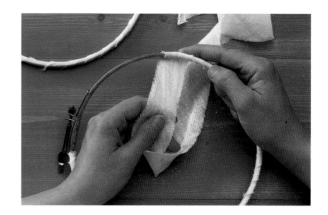

STITCHING

Cross stitch is usually worked between the threads of the fabric, and the threads counted to keep the stitches a uniform size. Stranded cotton makes even stitches if each strand is separated and laid out side by side before being threaded on to the needle. This is done by perfectionists but most of us run the needle between the strands to separate them, although they sometimes twist back on themselves. Do not cut over-long lengths of thread – about 46 cm (18 in) is plenty. Taping a snippet of thread alongside each colour on the chart key will help you follow the chart. It is a good idea to thread up several needles at once if you want to save time.

On the chart every coloured square, or square filled by a symbol, represents a cross stitch. The uncoloured squares represent the background fabric. Start working the cross stitch from the centre of the design, noting that the centre on some of these charts is the visual centre rather than the mathematical centre. Broken lines on the chart indicate a repeat pattern.

STARTING AND FINISHING

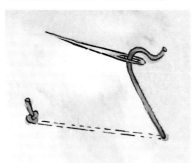

1 To start, make a knot near the end of the thread. Insert the needle from right side to wrong side a few stitches in the direction of work from where you want to make the first stitch.

2 Bring the needle to the right side and make complete stitches, covering the long strand that's on the wrong side, until you reach the knot on the surface of the work.

3 Snip off the knot close to the fabric and proceed. To fasten off, run the thread underneath a similar number of stitches on the wrong side.

MAKING A CROSS STITCH

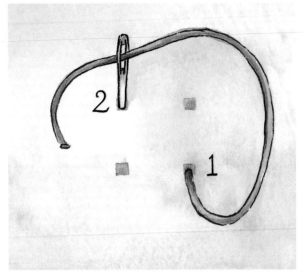

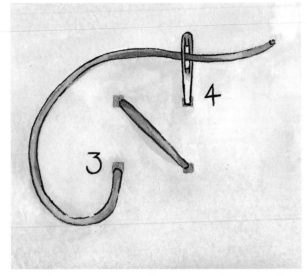

1 Working over two intersecting threads of fabric or one block of Aida weave, bring the needle out bottom right (1) and then insert it top left (2).

2 When the thread has been pulled through and the first diagonal made, bring the needle out bottom left (3) and then insert it top right (4) to complete the stitch.

WORKING BLOCKS OF CROSS STITCH

Blocks of cross stitch in a single colour can be worked as diagonals in one direction and completed with the second diagonals being worked on the return row. There is no fixed rule about the direction the top diagonal should take, but the work must be consistent. The back of the work should consist of short vertical stitches and not long diagonals. Single stitches should be completed before moving onto the next stitch.

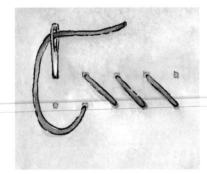

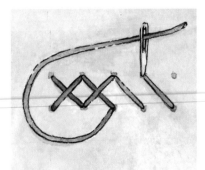

1 Work the first diagonal of each stitch along the row.

2 Then the second diagonals can be completed as you return along the row.

PRESSING

To press the finished work, place the stitching right side down on a padded surface and pin around the edge, squaring up the weave of the fabric if this has become distorted. Spray lightly with water or cover with dampened muslin. Using a warm iron, press out any creases putting very little pressure on the stitches. Remove the pins. If the stitching covers the whole surface of the fabric, press gently on the right side.

WASTE CANVAS

Double-mesh waste canvas is used to keep the cross stitches uniform when the fabric being stitched is not open-weave. This way, almost any fabric can be used for cross stitch.

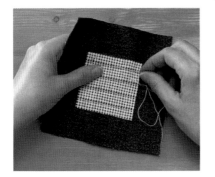

1 Tack (baste) a piece of waste canvas, slightly larger than the area to be stitched, onto the fabric. Make sure there will be plenty of canvas around the design once it is completed.

2 Work the cross stitch over the canvas and through the fabric, using the double-mesh canvas as a guide. The threads of the canvas must not be pierced by the needle, and when making adjacent stitches make sure the needle passes through the same hole in the fabric and does not leave split threads between stitches.

3 Once completed, remove the tacking (basting) stitches and trim the canvas close to the cross stitch. Dampen the canvas by spraying with water – the stitches will also be dampened but this does not matter. The water will dissolve the glue holding together the threads of the canvas. Use tweezers to pull out the waste canvas, one thread at a time.

STITCH SIZE

Both these motifs measure 14 stitches to 2.5 cm/1 in but the one on the right is worked over two strands of 28-count linen, while the one on the left is worked over a single thread of 14-count Aida.

These two motifs are also identical in number of stitches but they are different in size because of the different counts of fabric used. The threads chosen are appropriate to the scale of the fabrics.

CHARTS

HOME SWEET HOME

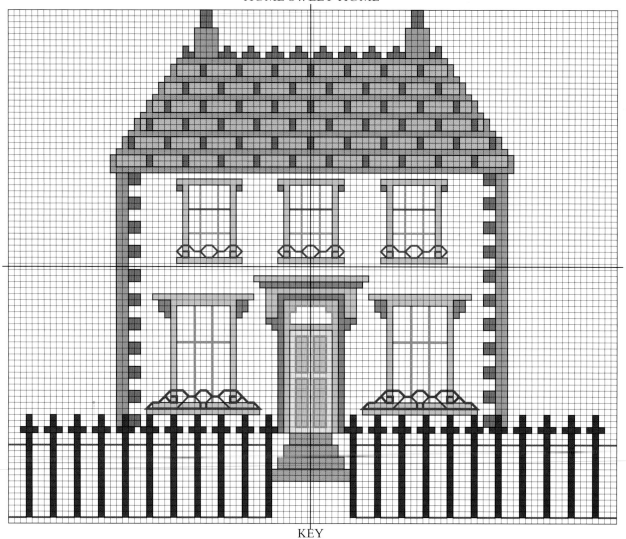

KEY

DMC Stranded Cotton

3816 pale green	535 dark grey	783 golden yellow
500 dark green	3799 charcoal grey	742 yellow
647 pale grey	3721 rust	500
414 mid grey	921 orange	3799

TIN CAN TREASURE

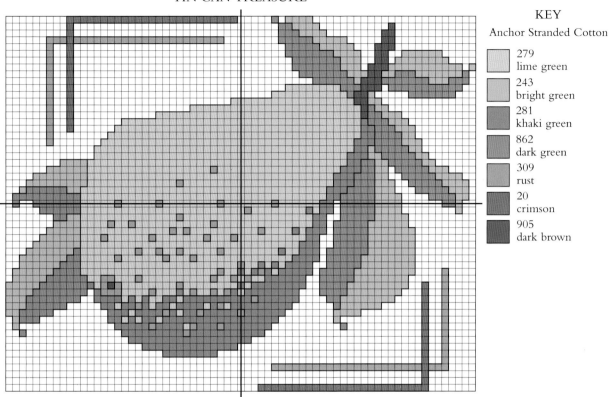

KEY

KEY

Anchor Stranded Cotton

279 lime green

243 bright green

281 khaki green

862 dark green

309 rust

20 crimson

905 dark brown

PISCINE PINCUSHION

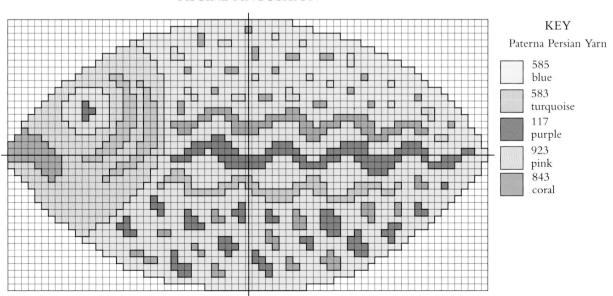

KEY

Paterna Persian Yarn

585 blue

583 turquoise

117 purple

923 pink

843 coral

SEASON'S GREETINGS

GARLAND

CHERUBS

GAME OF TAG

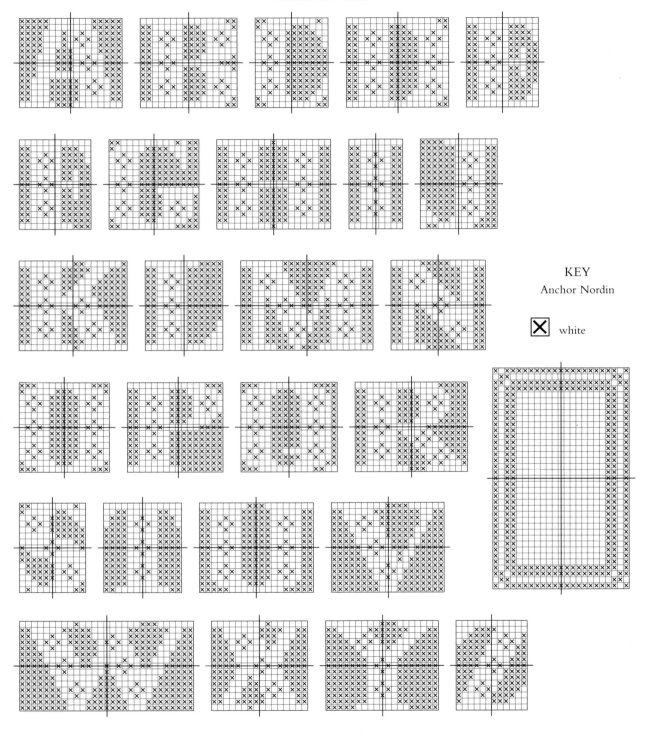

KEY

Anchor Nordin

☒ white

OFF THE PEG

KEY
OFF THE PEG
DMC Stranded Cotton

3808
green

304
red

KEY
SHELF LIFE
DMC Stranded Cotton

911
emerald green

907
bright green

986
dark green

470
olive green

918
rust

900
orange

3821
yellow

SHELF LIFE

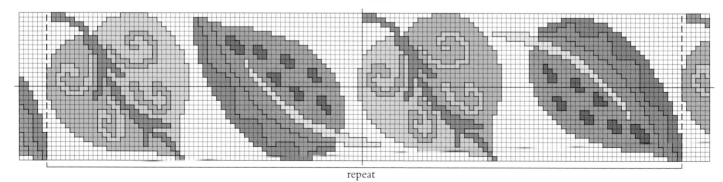

repeat

76

HEART APRON

KEY
Anchor Nordin

47
red

PLACE SETTING

KEY
PLACE SETTING
DMC Flower Thread

2823
navy

2321
red

CAKE RIBBON

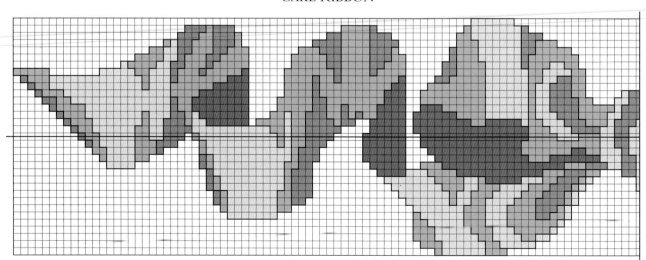

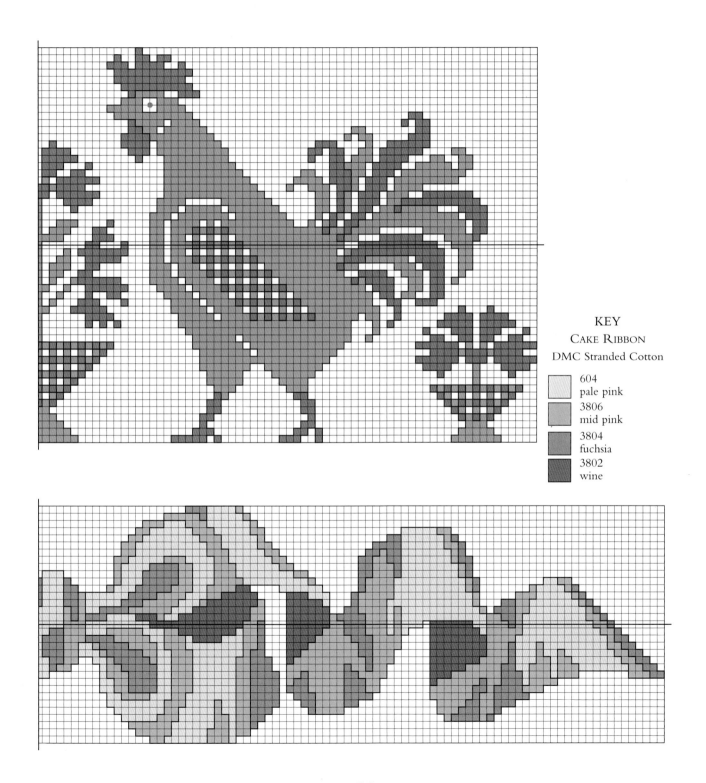

KEY

CAKE RIBBON

DMC Stranded Cotton

604
pale pink

3806
mid pink

3804
fuchsia

3802
wine

LEAFY PORTFOLIO

KEY
DMC Stranded Cotton

472
pale green
907
yellow-green
906
bright green
320
blue-green
904
dark green
936
olive green
3790
light brown
3021
dark brown

CURTAIN CALL

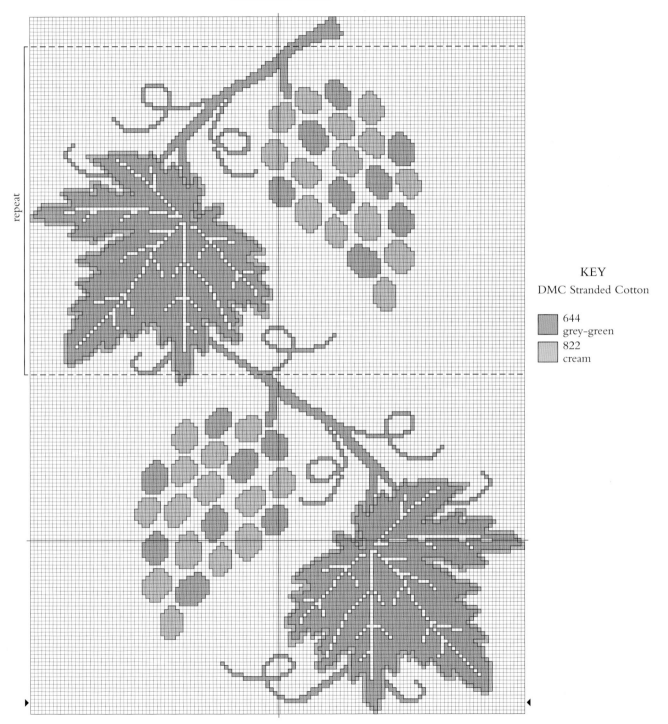

repeat

KEY
DMC Stranded Cotton

644
grey-green

822
cream

PERSONALIZED TABLE LINEN

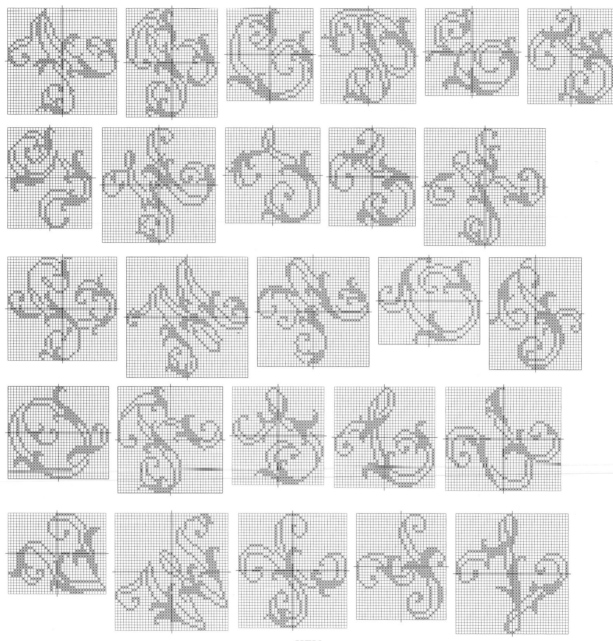

KEY

DMC Flower Thread

 white

FRUIT FLAVOURS

CHERRIES

STRAWBERRIES

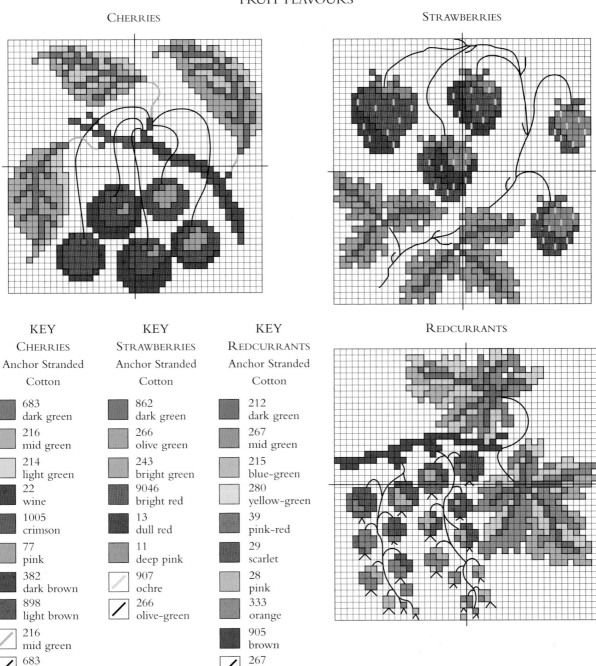

REDCURRANTS

KEY	KEY	KEY
CHERRIES	STRAWBERRIES	REDCURRANTS
Anchor Stranded	Anchor Stranded	Anchor Stranded
Cotton	Cotton	Cotton

	CHERRIES		STRAWBERRIES		REDCURRANTS
	683 dark green		862 dark green		212 dark green
	216 mid green		266 olive green		267 mid green
	214 light green		243 bright green		215 blue-green
	22 wine		9046 bright red		280 yellow-green
	1005 crimson		13 dull red		39 pink-red
	77 pink		11 deep pink		29 scarlet
	382 dark brown		907 ochre		28 pink
	898 light brown		266 olive-green		333 orange
	216 mid green				905 brown
	683 dark green				267 mid green

TRADITIONAL
SAMPLER

KEY
Anchor Stranded Cotton

	874 yellow
	858 sage
	217 green
	860 khaki
	875 acqua
	840 spruce
	850 teal
	1033 blue
	1016 rose
	895 coral
	897 wine
	889 umber
	382 dark brown
	926 cream

84

SHOO FLY COVER

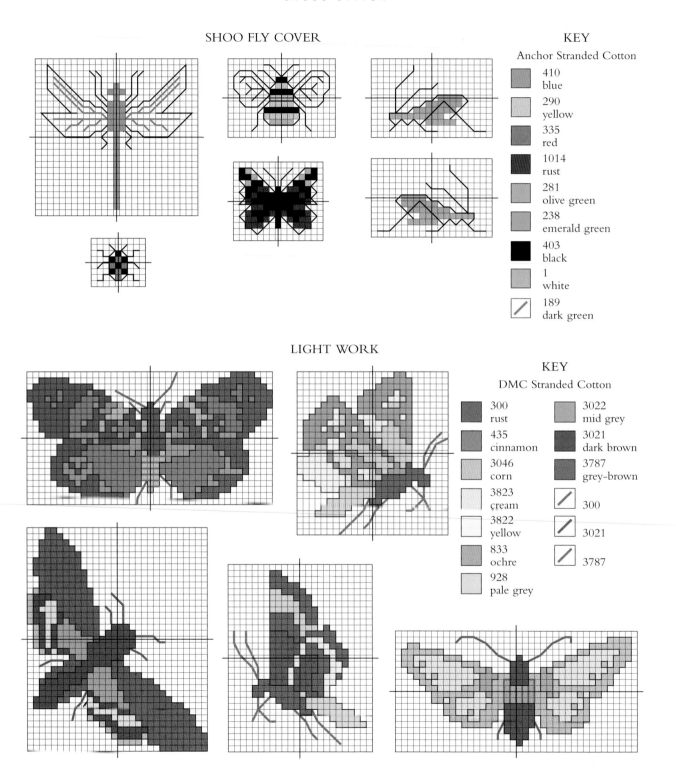

KEY
Anchor Stranded Cotton

410 blue

290 yellow

335 red

1014 rust

281 olive green

238 emerald green

403 black

1 white

189 dark green

LIGHT WORK

KEY
DMC Stranded Cotton

300 rust

435 cinnamon

3046 corn

3823 cream

3822 yellow

833 ochre

928 pale grey

3022 mid grey

3021 dark brown

3787 grey-brown

300

3021

3787

ALL SET FOR BED

KEY
Anchor Stranded Cotton

117
pale blue

176
mid blue

941
dark blue

SILK THROW

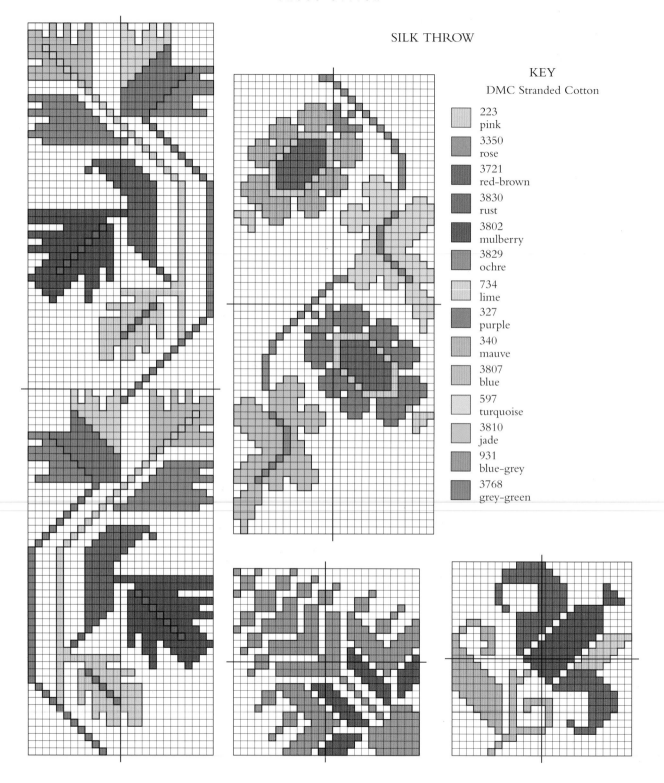

KEY
DMC Stranded Cotton

223
pink

3350
rose

3721
red-brown

3830
rust

3802
mulberry

3829
ochre

734
lime

327
purple

340
mauve

3807
blue

597
turquoise

3810
jade

931
blue-grey

3768
grey-green

SHIPSHAPE

KEY
Anchor Nordin

 127
navy
147
blue

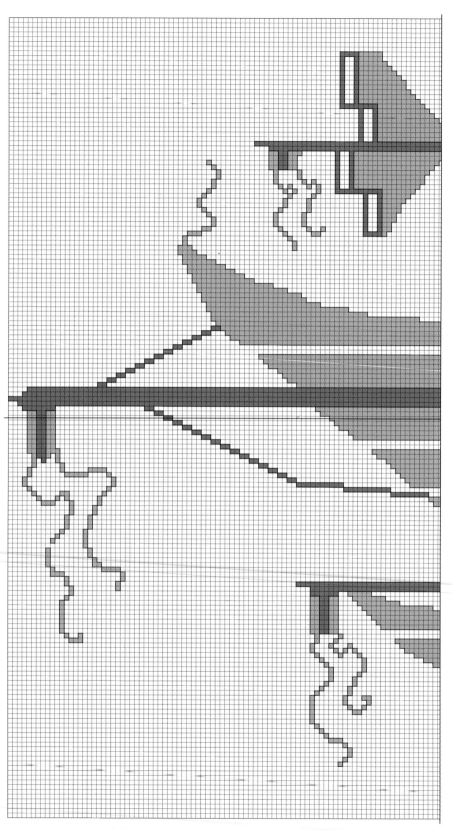

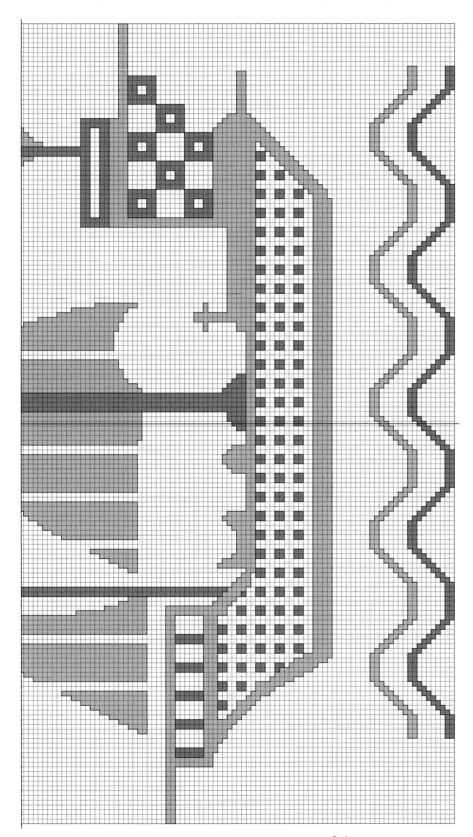

DENIM ROSE

KEY
DMC Soft Cotton

- 2570 wine
- 2572 dusty pink
- 2326 deep pink
- 2309 fuchsia
- 2986 bottle green
- 2561 dark green
- 2905 mid green
- 2562 grass
- 2563 apple green
- 2564 pale green
- 2743 yellow
- 2766 ochre

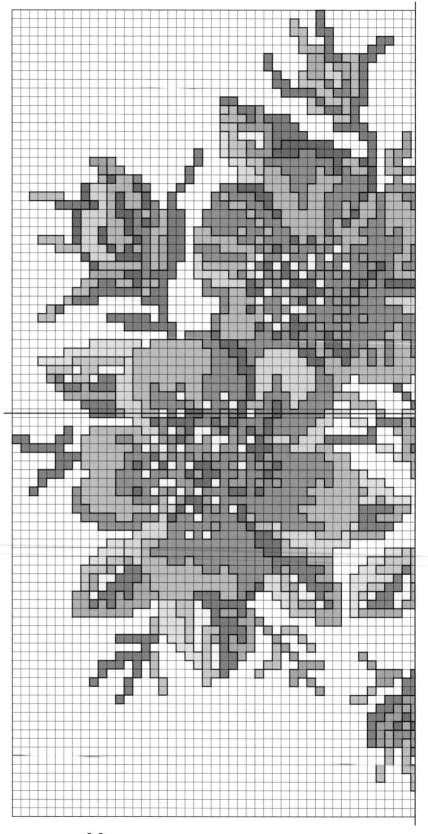

93

TURKISH CHAIR COVER

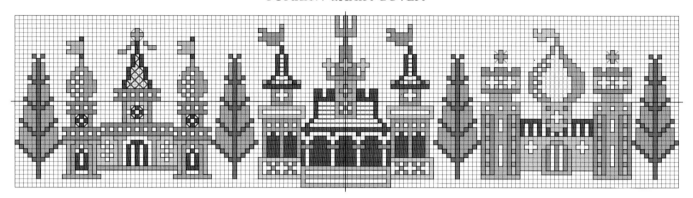

KEY

Anchor Coton à Broder 16

338
pink

307
yellow

341
rust

268
green

152
navy

169
mid blue

168
pale blue

307

341

A FINE LINE

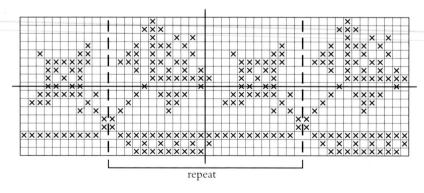

repeat

KEY

Anchor Coton à Broder 16

 black

SUPPLIERS

Most of the materials in this book can be obtained from good craft shops or haberdashery departments. Listed below are some of the suppliers included in this book.

UNITED KINGDOM

Coats Crafts UK
PO Box 22, The Lingfield Estate
McMullen Road, Darlington
Co. Durham DL1 1YQ
Tel: 01325 394394
Charter Craft fabrics, Aida and embroidery threads

DMC Creative World Ltd
Pullman Road, Wigston
Leicestershire LE18 2DY
Tel: 0116 2811040
Zweigart fabrics, Aida, linen bands, waste canvas and threads

Ian Mankin Ltd
109 Regents Park Road, London NW1
Tel: 0171 722 0997
Striped and natural fabrics

John Lewis
(branches throughout the country)
Haberdashery, threads and fabrics

The Linen Cupboard
21 Great Castle Street, London W1
Tel: 0171 629 4062
Tea towels and hand towels

Habitat
(branches throughout the country)
Linen and tea towels

The Silk Society
44 Berwick Street, London W1
Tel: 0171 287 1881
Silk matka

Wolfin Textiles Ltd
64 Great Titchfield Street
London W1
Tel: 0171 636 4949
Cotton Homespun and sheeting

AUSTRALIA

Coats Patons Crafts Pty Ltd
89–91 Peters Avenue, Mulgrave
Vic 3170
Tel: 1800 801 15

DMC Needlecraftt Pty Ltd
51–55 Carrington Road
Marrickville, NSW 2204
Tel: 02 559 3088

CANADA

Coats Patents
1001 Rose Lawn Avenue, Toronto
Ontario M6B1B8
Tel: 416 782 4481

CANADA AND USA

DMC Corportation
Port Kearny, Building 10
South Kearny, NJ 07032
Tel: 201 589 0606

USA

Coats and Clark Inc.
30 Patewood Drive, Suite 351
Greenville SC 29615
Tel: 864 234 0331

ACKNOWLEDGEMENTS
We would like to thank the contributors who designed the projects: Betty Barnden, chair cover and food cover; Penny Boylan, pincushion and shelf edging; Shirley Bradford, bedlinen and hand towel; Melody Griffiths, gift cards, portfolio, apron, sampler and jam pot covers; Gaye Hawkins, bag; Lesley Stanfield, cake band, tag, table linen and throw; Caroline Sullivan, picture and can; Dorothy Wood, cushion, curtain, lampshade, mat and peg bag, and Liz Gunner for all her help.

INDEX